Amazon FBA
Private Label
Step by Step

Exactly How to Start Your Own FBA Private Label Brand.
A Step by Step Guide to Selling on Amazon for Beginners.

Red Mikhail

[With Bonus Product Evaluation Checklist
and Supplier Cheat-Sheet Included Inside]

OTHER FBA BOOKS

AMAZON FBA Step by Step – to help you get started with Amazon FBA and arbitrage (the basics)

FBA Product Research 101 – an in-depth guide to product research

Amazon Keyword Research 101 – an in-depth guide to Amazon keyword research

FBA Product Sourcing Blueprint – a step by step blueprint on sourcing products and shipping it to Amazon/your preferred destination

Amazon FBA Sales Boost – 33 little tricks to triple your Amazon sales

Million Dollar Ecommerce – how to build an ecommerce brand outside Amazon.

These are also available as audiobooks.

You can find the whole series here:

https://www.amazon.com/gp/product/B086QZCJQQ

TABLE OF CONTENTS

Introduction

Welcome to another installment of the Amazon FBA Business Series where I show people how to create their own e-commerce business from scratch.

If you got the chance to read my other books, you know that I'm a no non-sense, no B.S. kind of guy. I write as if you're here talking to me in my living room and we just go straight to the point. And that's what you should expect from this book. A manual that can help you start and grow your own brand from scratch.

Who Is This Book For?

If you're someone who's just getting started with e-commerce, then this is for you.

If you're tired of buying courses after courses and you're ready to finally take action, then this is for you.

If you want a simple but step by step guide to launching your own private label brand, then this is for you.

If you have a little bit of capital to invest (I'd say at least $1,000), then this is for you.

And most importantly, if you care more about ACTIONABLE information than theory, then I'm your guy and this book is definitely for you.

Here's an overview of the step by step process of launching your own private label brand:

In **Chapter 1 - Account Setup & Your Business Foundation**, we'll talk about how to set up your Amazon Seller account and the requirements needed for you to start selling on Amazon. We'll also discuss some foundational stuff like mindset, capital allocation, and the main difference between a brand and a product. By the end of chapter 1, you'll have a clear path to starting an Amazon business that you know will still exist 3, 5 or even 10 years from now.

In **Chapter 2 - Product Research Like a Pro**, I'll show you exactly how to come up with product ideas that are more likely to sell. We'll talk about the criteria that I recommend every beginner should follow when researching products. We'll also discuss my top five product research methods plus I'll show you some examples on how to actually do these in real life (yup, no theory here, just pure actionable, "copy-able" stuff). You'll also receive a product evaluation checklist that you can use to evaluate whether a product is good to sell on Amazon or not. (This is an evaluation tool tailored fit for new Amazon sellers.)

In **Chapter 3 - Product Sourcing & Shipping for Beginners**, I'll show you 5 of the best ways to source your products and teach you exactly how to make your first order. *How do you make the first approach? How do you negotiate? How do you evaluate this supplier?* It's all here in this chapter.

We'll also discuss the shipping process so you'll know exactly how to ship the product from wherever you source it to Amazon's FBA warehouses ready to start making money for you.

In **Chapter 4 - How to Create an Amazon Product Listing,** we'll discuss the most important parts of your product listing and I'll teach you how to set it up so you can start getting orders on Amazon. I'll also give you some examples so you'll have a clear understanding on how to create each part of the listing.

In **Chapter 5 - Product Launch**, I'll give you a step by step instruction on how you can do a product launch so your product will have the momentum that it needs to start getting consistent sales month-in and month-out.

In **Chapter 6 - Amazon PPC for Beginners,** I'll show you the best way to get started with Amazon PPC. You'll learn how to set up your ads, how to evaluate ad results, and how to adjust based on the data you were given. Amazon PPC is one of the best ways to immediately start getting sales and start ranking higher on Amazon's best-seller and its search engine. By including a bit of Amazon PPC as part of your marketing strategy, you'll be able to directly reach buyers instead of just viewers. Unlike other ad platforms, people visit amazon.com to buy products – this alone makes running ads much more advantageous for your business.

■■

If you're already getting weak on your knees, scared of how much work needs to be done to start, launch, and grow an e-commerce business, then you should probably stop reading now. There are other much easier businesses for you. However, if you're one of the readers who's now ready to take a plunge in this business and give it a good try, then I urge you to read on.

Chapter 1 - Account Setup & Your Business Foundation

Let's start with the boring mundane stuff so we can get this out of the way. To get started with Amazon, you need to have a Seller's Account.

Two Types of Account:

Individual

The Individual account is free but you can only sell up to 40 items per month. In addition, you'll get charged $0.99 per item sold as part of the Amazon fees.

Professional

The Professional account is $39.99 per month and you can sell an unlimited number of items.

You can register here:

https://sell.amazon.com/

REQUIREMENTS

Here are some of the requirements to get your account verified:

A - Store Name – You want your store name to be the name of your brand. For your brand, think about a name generic enough to be in any category. If you already have a rough idea of what products you want to sell, you may want to veer in that direction and name a brand related to those niches.

(Note: Your brand name is not the name of your registered LLC or any business entity)

B – Bank Account Information

C – EIN (for tax purposes)

D – Driver's License or Passport (government valid I.D.)

E – Bank Statement

F – The Legal Stuff

Most people will advice that you start selling even without a business and just get started as an individual – and in most cases, they would be right. But if you want an additional peace of mind, then I highly recommend that you register a business even before you start selling anything. Registering as a business allows you to separate your individual assets to your business assets. If god forbid, you get sued, then they can only go after your business assets - and your personal assets will be safe.

I recommend using Legalzoom.com for registering your LLC. It's just a few hundred bucks and it's well worth the price you'll pay for it.

If you're an international seller, I recommend that you register as corporation or LLC in your country and create a bank account that accepts both USD and your local currency. Using Payoneer may also work since they can act as your U.S. bank and accept the payments in your behalf.

QUICK TIPS:

Quick Tip #1: In your Inbound settings, change it from Distributed Inventory Placement to Inventory Placement Service so your freight forwarder will only ship into one FBA warehouse. This saves you time and money overall.

Quick Tip #2: Change your advertising payment method into a business credit card to earn cash back.

Quick Tip #3: I heard rumors that Amazon refund pro accounts that are not actively selling anything. It may be different from case to case but I recommend that you message them if you ended up not using your pro account for a few months.

Your Business Foundation - Build a Brand Not a One Hit Wonder Business

With so much growth e-commerce is experiencing nowadays, it's easy to become one of those "one product wonder", get super lucky, and make thousands (even millions) just from that one product. But that doesn't always happen and relying on luck alone is NOT the type of business success you want to have. I'm not gonna lie, building a brand takes a lot more effort and focus. It's definitely harder to do and it requires a lot of short-term sacrifices. If you're willing to do the work NOW, then I 100% believe that you will succeed.

The Difference Between a Product and a Brand

Simply put, **a product is just one good idea**. *For example, a fidget spinner was a good idea back in 2016-2017 but it ended up being just one of those fads.*

A brand is a series of products targeting the same exact person. *For example, beautybakerie offers a line of products specifically targeting black women. They offer lip gloss, eye liner, concealer, primers, etc. That is a brand focusing on just one target market and offering a set of related products for their customer.*

A brand is crucial because it helps you differentiate your business from the market, and it makes the buying decision easier for your potential customers.

Another awesome thing about having a brand is you get to increase each customer's value. By offering a line of products, you'll have higher order value per customer since they will have lots of product variations and complementary items to choose from.

Heck, even this book series about FBA/Ecommerce is a BRAND. One book is a product, but this series of books is a brand. I can tell you with certainty that this series will be making more money 24 months from now that it does today. Why? Because I can release more books and create other products for the readers to buy.

It's the same with physical products, the more (high quality) complementary products you release, the more likely you are to increase your income.

How Much Capital Do You Need?

Unless you're already a mega successful person just looking for something to do, then I would assume that you have limited capital. For simplicity's sake, I would also assume that you have less than $5,000 to invest in this business. That $5,000 could also be big or small depending on the type of product you'll eventually choose to source. For example, if you choose a product that cost $2 per piece with a minimum order quantity of 1,000 – then you're gonna need $2,000 to complete that order. But wait a minute, you still need to pay for shipping and other expenses for doing business. In this case, you need to have at least double that amount so you can be safe.

Now, what if you don't have any money right now?

Should You Borrow Money to Fund Your Business? You probably shouldn't. If you really don't have money to invest, then I recommend that you get a part-time job or offer some freelance services instead. I don't want you to drown into debt by risking it all in this business.

Tracking Your Income and Expenses

It kills me that lots of people are starting their own ecommerce businesses but they never really track the money that's coming in and out of their pocket. The problem is Amazon accounting is inherently difficult.

There's almost no fixed fees except for the Pro Account membership fee.

Here's How to Get Started:

The simplest way to get started is to track your income and expenses in the macro level.

For now, just create a DEBIT/CREDIT or INCOME/EXPENSE line via an excel file and just put anything that comes in as INCOME and everything that comes out as EXPENSE. The most important thing here right now is to know whether you have enough capital to survive the next few months.

After a few months, start hiring a bookkeeper or an accountant to handle all of these for you. You don't want to spend too much time on this as focusing on other parts of your business will be more beneficial in growing your income. However, you also don't want to ignore it completely. Hiring someone to manage this for you is well worth the price because you'll always be aware of the financial health of your business. If you're going to hire a bookkeeper, try to hire someone with experience in Amazon accounting or ecommerce in general.

Chapter 2 - Product Research Like a Pro

This is probably one of the most exciting part of running a private label business. This is the part where we try to find products that we can sell on Amazon for a profit. In your case, you shouldn't just be after any product that will make money. The truth is a lot of product will do that for you. However, I do recommend that a beginner FBA seller follow the product criteria I'm gonna lay out in this chapter. By following what I call the "beginner criteria" you'll have a much higher chance of success and the opportunity to expand beyond a few thousand dollars in profits per month up to six or even seven figures per year.

So instead of asking, "What's a Good Private Label Product Anyway?"…
The real question you should be asking yourself is "What's a good product label for a beginner like me?"

This is the criteria I recommend you follow.

BEGINNER CRITERIA:

#1 - Your Own Interest/Experience

Do you have any interest in this niche? Are you the target market? The reason why I'm putting this as part of the criteria is because I want you to start a business where you care about the people you are serving. For example, if you've experienced first-hand what's it like to have braces (teeth) then you are more likely to find better solutions for this market. For an instance, I wear braces and I know how hard it is to wear them especially for people who has terrible gag reflex like me. Now, I don't have a solution for this at the moment but I wouldn't know about this problem in the first place if I'm not the target market. Having some kind of experience or interest in the niche you are selling in makes work a little bit more fun.

#2 - Less Than $50 on Amazon.com (optional but recommended)

For beginners, I recommend cheaper products that currently sells for $50 or less on Amazon. The reason I want you to sell slightly cheaper products is because they sell faster than expensive ones which gives you: a.) the cashflow that you need to operate the business and b.) the experience that you need to get better at operating the business.

#3 - Lightweight and Relatively Small (Easy to Ship)

Shipping has gotta be one of the most expensive parts of running a physical product business. To sell via FBA, you have to ship your product from China (or whatever country your product originated from) to Amazon's warehouses in the U.S. That usually cost a ton of money especially if you're shipping by AIR. So in the beginning, we want to avoid products that are heavy and large. My general idea for this is *if you can't put it in your average size backpack, then it is large. And if you can't carry it in one hand, then it is heavy.*

#4 - The 5X Rule

This rule has saved my butt countless of times. By following this rule, I was able to avoid products that I thought are bangers but on second look turns out to be duds.

The 5X rule is pretty simple. It states that you should be able to sell your products for 5x the original manufacturing cost (per piece) to at least break even.

For example, if a product cost you $3 per piece to source, then you have to be able to sell it for at least $15 on Amazon.

Following the 5x rule allows you to be on the safe side. Remember, you still have to pay for shipping fees, FBA fees, and other fees related to running your business. If you can't sell that product on Amazon for 5x what it originally cost you to produce it, then you probably won't make huge profits from that specific product unless you can sell hundreds of thousands in quantity.

#5 - Potential for Brand Expansion

Another important one is the potential for brand expansion. You should be able to launch other products complementary to your first one. Launching other products related to your original one not only allows you to make more profits but it also serves the market better by giving them more of what they want and need.

#6 - Non-Seasonal (Optional)

Personally, I prefer to sell products that are non-seasonal. This means that it should sell consistently throughout the year. Now, if you're willing to take a hit every few months or so and then have a surge every now and then, then feel free to target seasonal products. Seasonal products can be products related to Christmas, Halloween, New Year's Day, 4th of July and other culturally important holidays.

Seasonal could also mean the literal weather like snow season, summer, winter, and fall.

#7 - Value Skew Potential (Non-Optional)

This is the criteria that I NEVER want you to skip.

Value Skewing basically means **product improvements.**

You should pick a product that you can still improve upon. By doing this, you'll be able to separate yourself from the thousands of other sellers out there. This is best describe with an example so I'll expand more on this on the next part of the chapter.

#8 - Supplier Availability

Never, ever rely on just one supplier. The product you are sourcing should have multiple suppliers available just in case your first one defaults or fails in producing what they promised to produce. You do not want to be in a position where your product can only be made by one supplier. This doesn't give you any leverage and you'll be solely at their mercy when it comes to product availability.

#9 - Non-Electronic

If you're just getting started, I highly recommend that you stay away at electronically powered products. There's just so many things that can go wrong and they are generally much more expensive to source.

Note: You don't necessarily have to follow every single one of these criteria. At the very least, try to get at least 8 out of 10 before you proceed to sourcing that product.

REAL LIFE EXAMPLES:

Let me give you 2 examples of me running the criteria on 2 different products and I'll explain why it matches them or not.

Product #1 – Mouthguard for Teeth Grinding

The ConfiDental - Pack of 5 Moldable Mouth Guard for Teeth Grinding Clenching Bruxism, Sport Athletic,...

★★★★☆ ∨ 24,731

$14.97

#1 - Your Own Interest/Experience

Although this isn't a 100% requirement, I do suggest that you pick a product that you have interest or experience in. Have you ever had the need to use a mouth guard? Have you had any problems with teeth grinding or even for sports purposes? If you do, then you can put a check on this criterion.

#2 - Less Than $50 on Amazon.com

This one cost around $13-$20 on Amazon.

The ConfiDental - Pack of 5 Moldable Mouth Guard for Teeth Grinding Clenching Bruxism, Sport Athletic,... ★★★★☆ ~ 24,814

DenTek Professional-Fit, Maximum Protection Dental Guard For Teeth Grinding, 1 Count ★★★★☆ ~ 5,557

Plackers Grind No More Dental Night Guard for Teeth Grinding, Blue 10 Count **10 Count** ★★★★☆ ~ 8,637

Neomen Professional Dental Guard - 2 Sizes, Pack of 4 - Upgraded Mouth Guard For Teeth Grinding, Anti Grindin... ★★★★☆ ~ 10,561

I would say that the goldilocks number when it comes to prices is around $30-$50.

#3 - Lightweight and Relatively Small (Easy to Ship)

On average, these mouthguards are pretty light and small so they would be easier and cheaper to ship.

#4 - The 5X Rule

I don't know the sourcing price of the product yet, so I can simply go to Alibaba.com and check for the average price.

21

I'll try to find something similar to the products I'm looking at on Amazon and then I'll make sure that the product can be source for at least 5x less than how much it sells for on Amazon.

It looks like I can source this for an average price of $1 each.

#5 - Potential for Brand Expansion

This is the part where this product sort of veers off our criteria. Sure, we can sell other variations of the product and that would be great for our bottom line, but ultimately, we won't have as much complementary products related to a mouthguard for sports or teeth grinding.

I will give an X on this one because it misses the mark quite a bit.

#6 - Non-Seasonal (Optional)

A mouthguard isn't really seasonal so I would put a check mark on this one.

#7 - Value Skew Potential (Non-Optional)

To find what I can improve on a product, I usually start with the negative reviews on Amazon. I will spend hours just reading reviews just so I can find the pain points of the market. *What are the things that needs improvement? What are people complaining about?*

By reading the reviews, I'll get to know what my customers want and need when it comes to that specific product.

For example, just by reading some of the 1-star reviews on the mouthguards I found on Amazon, I found out that these are their concerns:

1 – The mouthguard is too big
2 – It's too thick
3 – It's very bulky

Knowing these problems, I can create a product that solves these issues, mostly by offering more size options and a more accurate sizing guide.

#8 - Supplier Availability

We cannot 100% know this until we do our full supplier research but just by looking at Alibaba for 5 minutes, I can see that there are hundreds of potential suppliers for this product.

#9 - Non-Electronic

This is a non-electronic product, so it's great for beginners.

We got 8 out of 9 of the criteria for this product so this is something I would consider sourcing and selling on Amazon.

(Note: This is just an example and I am in no way telling you that you will make millions selling mouthguards on Amazon. Please don't be a lazy bum and do your own research ☺)

Product #2 – Hand Grips (Gym, Weightlifting, Cross Training)

Bear KompleX 3 Hole Leather Hand Grips for Home...
☆☆☆☆☆ - 2,607
$38⁰⁰ - $39⁰⁸

These hand grips are made of quadruple-stitched leather made for durability.

WOD Nation Barbell Gymnastics Grips Perfect for...
☆☆☆☆☆ - 1,942
$9⁹⁷ - $11⁹⁷

The leather on these grips is soft and formfitting, making for a comfortable grip.

JerkFit WODies Hand Grips with Wrist Wraps for...
☆☆☆☆☆ - 2,456
$39⁰⁵

Well-regarded for their durability, we loved that the gloves were also made of thick breathable f...

#1 - Your Own Interest/Experience

I personally go to the gym and lift weights 3x a week and I can tell you from experience that having a weightlifting hand grip is a great way to not only protect the hand but also increase the performance.

This is a good product to use especially if it is made using high quality materials that don't easily break.

#2 - Less Than $50 on Amazon.com

The prices have a huge variation here and it looks like it's between $20-$50 on Amazon.

I would say that the average price would be at around $35. That's a good goldilocks price perfect for the newbie seller.

#3 - Lightweight and Relatively Small (Easy to Ship)

This is a pretty small and light product so I would put a check mark on this criterion.

#4 - The 5X Rule

By doing a quick search on Alibaba, I found that the average pair would cost me around $4 to $7 depending on quality and product specifications.

Following the 5x rule, it'll still be a profitable product if we could sell it for at least $35 ($7 sourcing price x 5).

#5 - Potential for Brand Expansion

There is some potential for product expansion on the design side (colors, sizes, product aesthetic). We can also offer other products like knee support sleeves, elbow sleeves, compression leggings, and compression sleeve shirt.

#6 - Non-Seasonal (Optional)

This is non-seasonal since people do workout whether it's winter, spring, summer, or fall (*isn't that a song or something?*).

#7 - Value Skew Potential (Non-Optional)

When it comes to value skewing, I like to look at products that has a lot of negative reviews on Amazon. If all I see are 99% positive reviews, then there's probably no need for me to create another product in this market.

By browsing around Amazon, it does look like that this market segment is already well served.

+3 colors/patterns

Mava Sports Leather Hand Grips with Wrist Support - Pull Ups Gloves Great for Cross Training, WOD, Deadlifts,...
★★★★☆ - 386

+5 colors/patterns

Mava Sports Ventilated Workout Gloves with Integrated Wrist Wraps and Full Palm Silicone Padding...
★★★★☆ - 3,587

+40 colors/patterns

Cobra Grips PRO Weight Lifting Gloves Heavy Duty Straps Alternative Power Lifting Hooks Best for...
★★★★★ - 4,553

PULLUP & DIP Neoprene Grip Pads for Weightlifting [Set of 4], Workout Pads, The Alternative to Gym Workout...
★★★★☆ - 312
$10⁹⁰

However, that wouldn't stop me from looking at some of the negative reviews because there will always be something to improve on. I will still give this a check mark because we can still improve our version of this product and serve the market even better than our competitors.

#8 - Supplier Availability

There are hundreds of suppliers just on Alibaba alone.

#9 - Non-Electronic

This is a non-electronic product.

This product got 9 out of 9 in our criteria so I would highly consider sourcing and selling this product on Amazon.

(Note: This is just an example and I am in no way telling you that you will make millions selling gymnastic/weightlifting grips on Amazon. Please don't be a lazy bum and do your own research ☺)

Product Research Methods

#1 – Non-Gated Categories

Non-Gated means that these are the categories with less product restrictions. For example, it'll be harder to get approved selling a dietary supplement than a meme coffee mug. For your first brand, you may want to consider non-gated categories so you can get more experience first.

Here are some of the Gated Categories:

Media Players
Collectibles
Watches
DVD, Blue-Ray

And here are some of the semi-gated categories where you need to deal with additional restrictions to get approval from Amazon:

Supplement
Grocery
Gourmet
Automotive
Sexual
Personal Care
Health & Beauty

Cameras

Software

Video Games

What I suggest is you start your idea research by familiarizing yourself with the categories and the sub-categories available on Amazon. When I was just getting started, I would usually spend 10-15 minutes per day just browsing different sub-categories and I'd make a list of unique products that piques my interest.

#2 - Yo Problems, Yo Money

This is my favorite way of coming up with product ideas.

I would usually start with my own problems both big and small.

For example, here are some of the "problems" that occupies my mind for the last 4 weeks.

Proper Budgeting

Canker Sores

What Food to Eat During First Few Days of Brace Adjustment

How to Expand My FBA Book Series

Fun Date Ideas

It doesn't matter how small or big those problems are, just make a list and write it all down on a piece of paper.

Next, I'll ask myself:

Why do I still have these problems?

What solutions have I come up with to solve these issues?

What product am I using and why is it/why isn't it working?

Can I create a better product than what I'm already using?

Remember, depending on your perspective - problems are just opportunities in disguise.

#3 - Reverse Keyword Search (via Google)

Search for potential problems that you want to solve and just literally type the word "products" or "solution" after the main keyword.

For example:

"back pain products"

You can also type the keyword and add the word Amazon after it.

"back pain amazon"

I guarantee you that you will find lots of new product ideas that you never would have thought of by simply doing this exercise.

The key is to search for a potential problem and then do a reverse keyword search by adding terms like "products", "amazon", "ecommerce" "physical product", "shopify" and other ecommerce related terms.

#4 - Amazon New Releases

https://www.amazon.com/gp/new-releases

Try to find products that has 100s of reviews even if they're still at the new release phase. This means that this product is HOT and selling really well at the moment.

This is super simple and easy to do but effective nonetheless for finding new product ideas to consider.

#5 - Etsy Best-Sellers

I also usually use ETSY when I'm coming up empty with ideas. I would just browse around the best-seller list and find something that catches my interest.

https://www.etsy.com/market/best_selling_items

I recommend that you start with the best-seller list because those are the proven ideas with a *ready to buy* market.

Private Label Product Evaluation Checklist

As a reminder, before you start sourcing your product, I recommend that you run it through this product evaluation checklist. The more criteria you get to check, the better.

#1 – Personal Experience/Interest in the Niche

#2 - Less Than $50 on Amazon.com if Possible (but $100 max)

#3 - Lightweight and Relatively Small (Easy to Ship)

#4 - The 5X Rule (You Should Be Able to Sell the Product for 5X Your Original Sourcing Cost)

#5 - Potential for Brand Expansion (Complementary Products Availability)

#6 - Non-Seasonal (Optional)

#7 - Value Skew Potential (There's a Room for Product Improvement) (Non-Optional)

#8 - Supplier Availability (Multiple Suppliers are Available)

#9 - Non-Electronic (Non-Gated Categories are Easier for Beginners)

Chapter 3 - Product Sourcing & Shipping for Beginners

Now that you already have an idea of what potentially profitable product you want to sell, it's time to find suppliers who can consistently produce that product for you.

In this chapter, I'm going to show you 5 of the best ways to find suppliers After that, I'll show you how to evaluate those suppliers and make your first order. On the second half of the chapter, I'll also give you instructions on how to actually get those products from your supplier to Amazon FBA's warehouse. To top it off, I'll also give some of the best tips that you must follow for you to have a seamless time sourcing your products.

5 WAYS TO FIND PRODUCT SUPPLIERS

#1 – 1688.com

1688 is the "China version" of Alibaba (you're probably familiar with this). Most products on Amazon are probably sourced via Alibaba, 1688 however is mostly used by Chinese companies.

What I like about 1688 is there's normally no minimum order quantity and I am guaranteed the lowest price possible. In addition, I can be assured that I'm dealing directly with the manufacturer and not just some third party seller who brokers the deal for me.

1688 is in Chinese so you need to install the Google Translate extension on your chrome.

Once you have this installed, just click "Translate this page".

You will also notice that the prices are in Yuan, so I recommend that you have your Yuan to USD converter in hand. I just use the one available on Google.

Another thing that you need is the messaging app WECHAT. Some suppliers here won't speak to you in

English so you need the app to translate your messages for you.

And one last thing, you also need to use the Google Translate app on Google so you can search for your product in Chinese.

Once you have all of those recommended tools, you simply have to search for your product name on the search bar and start looking for potential suppliers.

You can try searching for English or Chinese which can sometimes give you different results. I recommend that you do both.

Once you found a potential supplier, create a list on excel where you can post the link to their store and save them for the moment. You may want to have at least 10 potential suppliers first before you start contacting them.

It will also be great if you could search for that product on Amazon and make sure that you can sell it for at least 5x the product sourcing cost.

If you see that a product like the one you saw on 1688 is available for $2 per piece, then it should be selling for at least $10 on Amazon for it to breakeven or make a profit.

#2 – TTNET.NET

If you want to find manufacturers from Taiwan, then TTNET is your best bet. It works pretty much just like any other platform. You search for your product and you look at the available suppliers.

Here are some of the best things to look out for when you're using TTNET.

A – Make sure that they are the manufacturer of the product.
B – Double check the address of their company if it actually exists.
C – Take the available price with a grain of salt. Meaning, they are ALWAYS negotiable.

Honestly, you will probably find less products here but I would still recommend that you check it out because this is where I found one of my best suppliers and I still work with them to this day.

#3 - https://home.hktdc.com/

If you want to go the Hong Kong route, then HKTDC is the best one for you. When you search for your products, try to limit your searches to the ones who are "**Verified**

Suppliers" and the nature of business should be **"Manufacturer."**

You can also limit the searches to whatever country you prefer by clicking on the dropdown menu on **Country/Region** and the **Factory Location**.

For the actual product search terms, I recommend adding the words "supplier" "manufacturer" and "private label" for you to get more specific search results.

The prices aren't always available so you need to contact them first which you have to do anyway so that's not a big deal here.

#4 – Alibaba

This is probably the most famous one and quite honestly, the most trusted one by most sellers. Most buyers here are NOT from China so suppliers expect to communicate in English,

One of the advantages of choosing Alibaba is you'll get to work with people who already fully understood how the "Fulfillment by Amazon" business works. They'll know the best shipping methods, the process, the labels needed, and all those little things that makes selling on Amazon a little harder for beginners.

If you want a supplier who is already dealing with sellers like you, then you might want to stick to Alibaba.

The downside is there will always be MOQ and the prices will probably be a little more expensive compared to 1688 and other platforms.

Another advantage of using Alibaba is the ease of use. The website is very user friendly and there's literally millions of products available here.

If you decided to use Alibaba, make sure that you only work with suppliers with Trade Assurance and verified status.

By doing this, you are less likely to deal with amateurs and the chances of you getting scammed is almost zero.

Supplier Types

☑ Trade Assurance

☑ Verified Supplier

You can check those boxes on the left side when you search for any product you want. (Please see image above)

#5 – GOOGLE

Yup, our good old friend Google.

When it comes to Google, it all boils down to what keyword terms you'll use.
To find suppliers, I recommend using any of the following search terms.

"product name" + "manufacturer"
"product name" + "manufacturer" + "country/state/city"
"product name" + "manufacturer" + "private label"
"product name" + "private label"
"product name" + "private label" + "manufacturer"
"product name" + "country/state/city"
"suppliers for" + "product name"
"product name" + "supplier"
"product name" + "own brand"
"product name" + "best supplier"

Examples:

Weightlifting Grips Manufacturer Idaho
Weightlifting Grips Private Label
Bamboo Toothbrush Supplier
Bamboo Toothbrush Supplier California
Bamboo Toothbrush Own Brand
Suppliers for Bamboo Toothbrush

I recommend that you find at least 5-10 suppliers before you make the first contact. *

FIRST CONTACT, ORDERING SAMPLES, AND SUPPLIER EVALUATION CHEAT SHEET

A - Making the First Contact

The first contact is one of the most important parts of building a long-term relationship with your suppliers.

These people get hundreds of messages every day and you have to make it known that you are legit and serious. In addition, you also have to know some additional details about the product so you can make an informed decision later.

Here's a sample email I would send:

Hi,

My name is Red, a lead product manager of X company. We're interested in expanding our product line and we would like to work with you long-term. Can you answer the following questions referring to this product? www.theirstorelink.com/product1

#1 – What is the estimated cost of the product per unit including custom packaging (+ our logo) with an order of 500 units, 1,000 units and 2,000 units?

#2 – Can you print our logo in your product?

#3 – Can you provide custom packaging solutions?

#4 – Can you put the UPC in the product?

#5 – Are you able to send a custom sample of the product and how much would you charge if it is sent via DHL or FedEx to the following address: Your address here

#6 - Do you do product customizations?

#7 – Can you ship the products directly to Amazon's warehouses? Do you have experience in this regard?

Thank you and I'm looking forward to hearing from you soon,

Red, Lead Product Manager at Ecom X Company

It's important that you ask these questions because it helps you pre-evaluate your potential suppliers. If they didn't reply within 3 days (or they never replied at all), then there's no way you should be making an order on their company. You want to use this as a test if they're actually easy to communicate with and if they actually understand how the whole business works. If they can't answer simple questions like these, then you shouldn't be working with them in the first place.

B - Ordering Samples

Once you did your pre-qualification (read the answer to your questions), I recommend that you narrow down your choices to 3 suppliers. Order some samples and choose the supplier with the highest quality product.

Unless you're 1,000% sure that the product is of the highest quality, I recommend that you ALWAYS order samples first before you go through your first order.

In addition, ask for product customization (if your product needs one) before you order a sample. You will most likely have to pay higher prices for this but it's totally worth it because you'll get to use and evaluate the product first-hand. Unless the only change your product has are logos and packaging, then it's an absolute must that you see a custom-made sample of your product before you make the initial order.

A Note on Negotiation:

If you're sourcing your products from 1688, then it is likely that you are already getting the lowest price. Try not to haggle too much unless your profits are really gonna get squeezed. For Alibaba and other platforms, I would say that there's more leeway for negotiation if you're dealing directly with the manufacturer. Remember that more units mean more negotiating power for you. If the MOQ you can afford isn't even in their acceptable range, then you will probably have to settle for slightly higher prices. The most important thing as a beginner is to get experience and to know how the whole process works. Once you go through the process a few times, you can now start focusing on increasing your profits.

C - Supplier Evaluation Cheat Sheet

You should have the details for all of these before you go through your order. You will get most of the information in the process of talking, researching and negotiating with your supplier.

1 – Name of Supplier

2 – All contact details (email, phone #, skype etc.)

3 – Website

4 – Complete business address

5 – Minimum order quantity (MOQ)

6 – What are their packaging and labeling options

7 – Do they do product customization?

8 – Lead time (the amount of time needed for them to complete the manufacturing of the product – excluding shipping time)

9 – Shipping Options/Methods

10 – Price quotes for MOQ

11- Price quotes for packaging/labeling/customization

12 – The volume of product they can create every month

13 – How does shipping works and what are the fees (from Manufacturer's factory to your warehouse /Amazon FBA - DOOR TO DOOR)

14 – Are there any additional FEES for everything? (shipping, tax, customs)

15 – Do they do inspections?

16 – The exact weight, height and every single specifications of that product

17 – What payment methods will they accept? Warning: Never ever pay via money transfer (Western Union). If they insist, run.

18 – Any possible third-party options for shipping, packaging, labeling and product customization?

ADD THE FOLLOWING IF YOU'RE SHIPPING DIRECTLY TO AMAZON FBA'S WAREHOUSE:

19 – Make sure that you print (in pdf) all the labels and send it to your supplier.

20 – Always inform your supplier that you are shipping directly to Amazon's warehouse.

HOW TO SHIP DIRECTLY TO AN AMAZON FBA WAREHOUSE

There are many shipping options but this is the path that I recommend you take.

If you're 100% sure about the quality of your product; you've seen the inspection and you trust your seller with all your hard-earned investment, then it's a good idea to just ship it directly to Amazon's FBA warehouse.

THE STEPS:

Step 1 – Understand What Labels You Need

To send the shipment directly to Amazon's warehouse, you will need the following:

A – UPC Code. This needs to be in all of your products and it is highly recommended that you use a box design.

B – Carton Label. This is the label that appears at the top of your Master Carton. This is the label that Amazon scans when it arrives in their warehouse.

C – FSNKU. This is an Amazon Specific Label and you need a UPC to get it.

Step 2 – Follow the Amazon Shipping Plan

1 – Go to your Sellers Central account.

2 – Go to Manage Inventory

3 – Choose the product box that you set up for your listing and then click on SEND/REPLENISH INVENTORY.

Step 3 – Setup the Ship from Address

Ask your supplier for their full address and input it in the ship from section.

Step 4 – Choose Your Packaging Type

Choose "case-packed products"

Case-packed products are items that has identical items that has matching SKUs, and each case must have the same number of products. Your supplier should already know how this works so make sure that you ask them about it.

Now, multiple cases can be packed into a larger box called Master Carton, which does not qualify as case-packed and must be split into cases.

Another thing to remember is the word "unit per case" – This refers to the number of items per case and NOT the number of cases per Master Carton.

Okay, this may all sound weird and complicated, but trust me – this will all make sense once you start to actually ship your items and once you start working with your supplier.

Step 5 – Set Quantity

The next step is to set the quantity of your product.

Step 6 – Go to "Prepare Products" section and then click on the show ASIN/FNSKU checkbox.

Next, choose "Merchant".

Step 7 – Click on Print labels for this page.

A pdf file will appear and this is the file that you should send to your supplier, to be included in the shipment itself. They will know what to do with this file as long as you clarify that this product goes directly to Amazon.

Step 8 – Review your shipment and choose SMALL PACKAGE DELIVERY or SPD.

Step 9 – Confirm the details that you input about your product (weight, numbers of units, etc.)

Step 10 – Print your box labels and then complete the shipment.

Make sure that you save the box labels that will appear and send that as well to your supplier.

You will get something similar to this image:

And that's it, you now have completed the process of shipping directly to Amazon's warehouse. Just send all the printed labels to your supplier and they will already know what to do with it.

If you need a more detailed instruction on how to deal with the FBA shipping and packaging, I recommend that you checkout Amazon's official guide in PDF form.

You can download it here: https://images-na.ssl-images-amazon.com/images/G/01/fba-help/QRG/FBA-Shipping-Inventory-to-Amazon.pdf

If that link didn't work, just Google search "Amazon FBA Shipping Guide PDF" and it should appear on the first page.

QUICK TIPS ON DEALING WITH SUPPLIERS

#1 – Ask Questions. Do not hesitate to ask questions to your supplier if you do not understand some things. Remember that they are dealing with sellers like you every single day and if they have been in this business for quite a while, then there's almost no scenario they still haven't experienced. Ask questions and they'll most likely know how to deal with your problems.

#2 – Do Not Assume Anything. Always put everything into a contract. I'm not a lawyer so I cannot give you legal advice, but the most important ones are: the price, the quantity, the lead time, and the action needed in terms of default in their part.

#3 – Negotiate But Don't Haggle. Treat your suppliers like long-term business partners (because they are). You may get a very low price just by sheer will but that kind of tactic won't lead to a long-term business relationship. It's better to pay a little higher now especially if your supplier is easy to work with. Focus on the long game and you'll actually have a more fun time working on your business and you'll save more money as they gave you more and more favorable deals.

#4 – Treat Everyone with Respect. Don't act like you're the master of the world and every single supplier is your slave. Always treat everyone with respect and always respect the culture they are coming from. For example, Chinese New Year is an important holiday for China and it is likely that you'll experience delay and late communication the week leading, during, and after the actual celebration. Don't get mad and raged – instead, you should just add the delay as part of your lead time so you can prepare in advance.

How long is the Chinese New Year? ⌃

sixteen days

Chinese New Year is celebrated for sixteen days (from **Chinese New Year's** Eve to the Lantern Festival). The preparations start seven days before **Chinese New Year's** Eve. Many celebration activities for this period are traditional customs, but some are quite **new**...

#5 – Calculate Your Profits

I recommend using this free FBA calculator tool so you know whether you're bound to make a profit or not.

https://junglescout.grsm.io/fbacalculator

(The instructions are also in that page)

Chapter 4 - How to Create an Amazon Product Listing

The listing only has one job, and that is to sell the product. Treat your listing as your salesman in print. Everything that the potential customer needs to know should be in that one little page.

In this chapter, I'm going to show you the parts of the listing, how to create them, and also give some examples of good ones to copy or get inspiration from.

PARTS OF THE LISTING

A – Title

Your title is the most important text on your listing. Your title should tell not only the customers, but also Amazon itself **what your product is**. That means the customers should easily identify what the product is just by reading the title. The title should also contain keywords that are highly relevant to the product you are selling. For example, Amazon will be happy to see the keyword "Ortho" and "Toothbrush" together. However, Amazon will frown upon overoptimizing and putting words like "best" "cheapest" and other subjective term in there.

Here are some title requirements that you need to follow:

A – Do not use any promotion terms like "for sale","sale", and "free".

B – Do not use any subjective terms like "cheapest", "only", and "best".

C – The title should not exceed 200 words

D – Do not put any unrelated keywords in the title. Amazon will not rank your listing if you do this. Keyword stuffing just for the sake of optimization is quite stupid. Imagine searching for "bamboo toothbrush" and seeing kitchen knives instead. That happens when sellers get greedy and put random words in their listing just for the sake of optimization.

E – Do not state the price of the product.

F – Do not use any special characters like "™", "@", and "®"

A Simple Title Formula:

Brand Name + Primary Keywords + Main Features

1 – Your **brand name** is the name of your company or your brand.

2 – Your **primary keywords** are the top 3 keywords that people search when they are looking for a product like yours. This one is pretty obvious and those keywords would likely be the same ones you used when it comes to searching for suppliers.

3 – The **main features** are the keywords that customers are typing on Amazon related to your primary keyword. You can find these features just by spying on your competitors and looking at their own titles.

In this example below, the primary keyword is: *Biodegradable Bamboo Toothbrushes*. And the features are: *10 Piece BPA Free Soft Bristles, Natural, Eco-Friendly, Green and Compostable*

> Biodegradable Bamboo
> Toothbrushes, 10 Piece BPA Free
> Soft Bristles Toothbrushes, Natural,
> Eco-Friendly, Green and
> Compostable
> Brand: Nuduko

Here's an example of a complete title optimized for customer sales and Amazon search ranking.

Ortho-Max | Biodegradable Bamboo Toothbrush | Eco Friendly, Soft Nylon Bristles, Organic Material, Smooth Handle, 100% Recyclable.

(Use a vertical bar to separate each part of the listing)

The Breakdown:

Brand Name - Ortho-Max

Primary Keyword - Biodegradable Bamboo Toothbrush

Features - Eco Friendly, Soft Nylon Bristles, Organic Material, Smooth Handle, 100% Recyclable

B - Bullet Points

Your bullet points are the info you see below the title.

About this item

- [ECO FRIENDLY AND BIODEGRADABLE]: Bamboo toothbrush made from natural sustainable Bamboo farms, our product is 100% Natural! Their quality is as same as your generic plastic brushes but biodegradable.
- [A PACK OF 10 TOOTHBRUSHES]: A pack of ten and each one is individually packaged in cardboard. It is very suitable for family member.
- [EASY TO USE]: No need to dry the bamboo handle after use, Use method the same as the plastic toothbrush.
- [SOFT BPA FREE BRISTLES]: The bristles are made from high-quality nylon which is soft, perfect for getting all the plaque off of your teeth.
- [100% SATISFACTION GUARANTEE]: If there have any problem please contact me, I will provide a perfect solution for you. we support refund within one month and replacement within three months.

Your bullet points have 2 primary tasks:

A – SELL THE PRODUCT. Highlight the features and benefits, show what is different about it, and show them how it will solve the customer's problem.

B – Add keywords relevant to your product to increase your Amazon rankings.

Requirements for Creating a Bullet Point:

1 – Use keywords in the beginning of the bullet point and then explain what it means. [Optional]

Please see example below.

- [ECO FRIENDLY AND BIODEGRADABLE]: Bamboo toothbrush made from natural sustainable Bamboo farms, our product is 100% Natural! Their quality is as same as your generic plastic brushes but biodegradable.

2 – Separate the keywords and the explanation with a semicolon.

[ECO FRIENDLY AND BIODEGRADABLE]: Bamboo toothbrush made from natural sustainable Bamboo

3 – Do not use symbols, periods, hyphens, questions marks, and any other special character.

Here's the formula I recommend for creating your bullet points:

Bullet #1 – Primary Feature + Benefits

The first line should be the most important feature. It should be the number 1 reason why most people buy whatever you are selling. For example, most people who buy bamboo toothbrushes want to protect the earth and save mother nature. If that's the case, then that's what I'm going to talk about in the first line.

Bullet #2 – More Features + Benefits

Line #2 is basically more of the same except you're gonna mention more product features and the benefits that they'll get along with it.

Bullet #3 – Differentiation

This is the part where you can mention any feature of your product that makes it different from the competition.

Bullet #4 – More Problems to Solve + the Solution

In line #4, I will give them a problem related to the product and then I'll boast about a feature that solves it. For example: *100% Biodegradable Packaging: Even the packaging is made of 100% recyclable material so you don't need to worry about polluting the Earth.*

Bullet #5 – Guarantees

This is the part where I offer a money back guarantee or any type of promises about the product.

Here's an example of a great product bullet:

- ★ GO GREEN! – Why fill up landfills with plastic when you don't have to? Help the environment, and feel better about your mark on this world with Bamboo Toothbrush! It's the ecological way to not only keep your mouth fresh for just as long as a normal toothbrush, but help the environment at the same time!
- ★ A PACK OF 4 TOOTHBRUSHES – will last one person a full year. Buy a pack of 4 toothbrushes for each person in your household.
- ★ SMOOTH & NATURAL BAMBOO HANDLE – will never splinter and is water resistant. Stronger and harder than wood, Bamboo is also more durable and healthier than any plastic. No need to dry the handle after use, just rinse your toothbrush and put back into its holder, just like you would with any other old plastic toothbrush
- ★100% RECYCLED BIODEGRADABLE PACKAGING – even the packaging is made in craft paper,no worry about it polluting the environment when you throw it away
- ★ GUARANTEED – We love this toothbrush, and we're sure you will to. However, if for any reason you don't, no worries! Just send it back our way for a full refund of the purchase price. It's natural quality with an unbeatable guarantee. Why keep looking when you've found your solution right here!

C – Product Description

I try to keep my product description to the bare minimum. In my opinion, its job is not to sell the product – that's the bullet, images, and the title's job. Most of my product description follow this formula:

Overview + Specs + Warranty and/or Guarantee

1 – Overview. I usually just rephrase my first bullet and give 1-2 sentences description of the product they are buying.

2 – Specs. This is the part where I make a bullet form list of the specs like weight, height, dimensions or any numbers that the customers might need to know.

3 – Warranty/Guarantee/Call to Action. This is where I reiterate that's there a guarantee or warranty available for the product (only write one if there's any). (You can also put some kind of call to action and ask for a purchase here).

Example:

New technology of bristle fixation
In the production of virgin forest bamboo toothbrush, we use a new bristle fixing technology without any glue. Please use it with confidence.

By ordering our toothbrushes you take care not only about your oral cavity but also about health of our planet.

We recommend storing toothbrushes in a dry place.

So, click "ADD TO CART" now before the stock runs out!

Specifications

Handle Length: 7.5 Inch

Brush head length: 1.1 Inch

Bristles length: 0.47 Inch

A paragraph style product description also works. Just make it short and easy to read.

Product description

Our Top Quality Bamboo Toothbrushes 8 Pack comes with two individual boxes of 4 nicely packed toothbrushes. Getting 8 Toothbrushes at a great value can get you a long way, and last at least a year. Our bristles are made from Soft, BPA Free Nylon Bristles which does a great job to remove tartar, and plaque to keep your teeth clean at all times. Your teeth will always remain healthy! Our toothbrush handles are made from Natural, Organic 100% Biodegradable Bamboo Handles. The curve shape of the bamboo handle fits great in your hand. The bamboo handle is very smooth and has no splinters. The bamboo handles are individually numbered so that you will never mix them up.

E – Product Images

Your product images are probably the most important part of your listing – tie with the title. Your images are their only "touch point" for the product and **your customers are going to assume that the quality of your product is directly proportionate to the quality of your listing images.**

ALWAYS use a professional product photographer – trust me they are worth every penny in the long-term. Also, only hire someone who specializes in product photography so you'll get higher quality shots.

Quick tip: Before you upload your images, change the file names of your photos to your main keywords. These file names will act as a metadata for Amazon thus increasing your chances of rank search for those keywords.

Example:

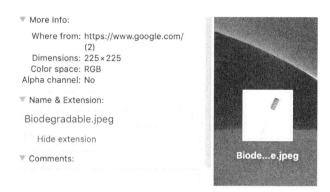

More Info:

    Where from: https://www.google.com/
                  (2)
    Dimensions: 225×225
    Color space: RGB
Alpha channel: No

Name & Extension:

Biodegradable.jpeg

   Hide extension

Comments:

F - Backend Keywords

Your backend keywords are the keywords you need to input on Amazon's metadata. This let Amazon knows that these are the keywords that you want to rank for.

For your backend keywords, I recommend using keywords that you got from your competitors' listings. Remember, only put keywords related to your product so you don't overoptimize and mess up Amazon's search engine.

Read this article for more info about this:

https://www.sellerapp.com/blog/amazon-backend-keywords/

A Note on Product Pricing

Pricing is pretty easy to navigate. Here's how you'll discover what price you should charge:

1 – Look at the competition. Look at similar products available on Amazon and price your product a bit lower than the competition at first. This will give you a bit of a sales boost especially if you don't have too many reviews yet.

2 – Look at your calculations. Your goal in the beginning is to at least get to the breakeven point. Lower your prices but make sure that you do your calculations and only price it to the point where you'll at least hit the breakeven point. After a few weeks or months when you already have more reviews, you can increase the price by at least 5% more every 2 weeks until you see the sales go down (that's when you stick to that price for a while).

Here's an FBA Calculator you can use:

https://junglescout.grsm.io/fbacalculator

3 – Test. The good news is you can always change the price of your product so there's no need get stuck with just one price forever. Always keep testing and try to do it in 4 to 6 weeks' timeline. You cannot get proper data if you only do it in less than 1 week. In addition, try not to change anything in your listing when you're testing the price. Only test 1 variable at a time so you won't mess up your data.

Resources

For the technical side of setting up a listing, I recommend that you checkout the following resources:

https://www.salesbacker.com/blog/77/How_to_set_up_yo ur_Amazon_product_listing

https://www.kaspien.com/blog/guide-to-creating-amazon-listings-in-seller-central/

https://sellercentral.amazon.com/gp/help/help.html?itemID=39EFY66ZLSJQ7PM

P.S. If you want a more detailed approach to keyword research and product listing optimization, check out my book **Amazon Keywords Research** available as eBook, paperback, or audiobooks everywhere.

Chapter 5 – The Minimal Product Launch

Here's the thing about product launches… they're not really 100% needed to build a successful FBA business. So why in the world am I still teaching it? The reason why is because I want you to start with momentum because most people reading this probably don't have a huge marketing budget at the moment. And that's why we need that initial momentum so we can get the ball rolling and get some organic sales as well after the initial launch.

2 Steps to Our "Minimal Launch"

Step 1 – Get the First 5-10 Reviews
Step 2 – Get Sales Momentum via Amazon PPC

Yup, that's it. The goal is to get some reviews and then paid sales via PPC. After that, we also want to get some organic sales which will happen only if we're also getting some sales via ppc. Each paid sale that we get increases our ranking and those increases in rankings get us more organic sales, *get it?*

In Amazon, the more sales you get, the more sales you get. As simple as that.

Step 1 – Get the First 5 Reviews

Here are some of the best ways to get your first 5-10 reviews.

Amazon's Early Reviewer Program

What it does is it allows you to get at least 5 initial reviews for your brand-new product.

But first, you have to find out if you are eligible for the program.

Here are some of the requirements according to Amazon:

- The product must be for sale on Amazon.com or Amazon.co.uk
- You have to have a brand registry
- The product must have less than 5 reviews when you apply for the program
- The product cost must be at least $15
- It must have its own SKU barcode

The Price

Is it worth the $60 that you have to pay for? I believe so. A product that has at least 5 reviews is 2.5x more likely to get sales than the one without any.

Go on and apply your product to the Early Reviewer Program because it's the best $60 you'll ever spend this week.

*To **participate**, submit your product via 'Seller Central > Advertising > **Early Reviewer Program**'. You can submit single SKUs directly via the **Amazon Early Reviewer Program** dashboard.*

Friends BUT NOT Family

Ask your friends to buy your product so they can post a "verified" review on Amazon. Now, do not ask your family members since they are likely using the same i.p. as you. Amazon can track this and it is 100% against Amazon's terms. Only ask friends that lives at least 10km away from you.

We'll discuss product reviews more later in the chapter, just know that those 2 are enough to get you that 5-10 initial reviews. Don't overthink it, just do it.

Step 2 – Get Momentum via Amazon PPC

Our launch strategy only requires 2 things: The first one is the reviews, and then the next one is Amazon PPC. The goal is to get your product to rank in the best-sellers and also into the top of page 1 for the most searched keywords of your product. Say you are getting PPC sales from the keyword "oat milk", then Amazon is going to reward you with higher search rankings which will also give you lots of non-ppc/organic sales.

PPC PRIMER:

The first week of our launch is where we spend most of our PPC budget. I would say that you need at least $500 to get amazing results and maybe $1,000-$1,500 if your product is price above $50. But don't worry about losing money. Think of this as a long-term investment for your brand. If you follow my instructions later, I'm 100% confident that you are going to get your money back and more.

The key with Amazon PPC are these 3: KEYWORDS, LISTING, PRODUCT.

Keywords - you need to target keywords that are highly relevant to your product. If you built your master keyword list and did your research, then by now, you already have what you need to launch a successful ppc campaign.

Listing – always optimize your listing first before you run a single campaign. Check your title, images, bullet points, and product description. Make sure that you follow the way I taught you how to create your listing.

Product – No amount of good ad copy or optimized listing will ever compensate for a bad product. If your product sucks, then customers will eventually turn on you and put bad reviews on your listing. If your product sucks, then you shouldn't be running ads in the first place. Heck, you shouldn't even be selling on Amazon at all.

TIPS BEFORE YOU DO PPC:

A – Make sure that you already have a list of keywords you want to target for your ads.

B – Make sure that you get at least 5-10 reviews first before you run your ads. Reviews are social proof that other people are actually buying your product as well.

C – Optimize your listing to maximize sales. (Read chapter 4 again)

We will discuss PPC more on the next chapter. The key for now is to understand its importance when it comes to our launch strategy. Without that initial PPC boost, it's going to be hard to get long-term organic sales and compete with the big boys in your industry.

AMAZON REVIEWS EXPLAINED:

In this part, allow me to discuss reviews a bit more.

Easily put, reviews are the ranking system used by Amazon customers. More positive reviews mean more social proof that you have a good product and hundreds if not thousands are also using your product. It's a vital part of running an ecommerce business and Amazon is constantly changing their policies about it, for the betterment of the customer of course.

Remember that Amazon only wants the best for the customers so authentic reviews are must haves and non-negotiable. I'd rather have 10 legit reviews from actual customers than 100 shady/fake ones.
Your reviews must NOT come from the following:

A – Someone with monetary interest in the company selling the product (you, co-founder, your employees)
B – Someone who has been incentivized to put the review
C – Someone connected to you by blood (family members)
D – Any Facebook friends (at least not via a link you sent them on fb, email your Amazon store link instead)

E – Facebook Reviewers Group
F – Anyone who has the same ip address as you
G – Anyone who has the same last name as you

Verified and Non-Verified Reviews:

A verified review weighs more heavily when it comes to Amazon rankings and it's something that customers will consider a more legit review.

⭐⭐⭐⭐⭐ **I just wanted a toothbrush.**
Reviewed in the United States on December 8, 2017
Size: 6 Count   Style: Soft   Verified Purchase

To get a verified review status, the customer must have purchased the product for at least 80% of the listing price.

Yes, verified reviews are hard to get nowadays…. It's so easy to just break Amazon's terms of service and just use "strategies" like giveaways and launch services. But these have always been in the grey area of doing business on Amazon. I would rather have you focus on creating a really good product that delivers real value to your customers. That is honestly the best way to get a review – PROVIDE MASSIVE VALUE, BRING A GREAT PRODUCT TO THE MARKET. There's no better way to get reviews than that. PERIOD.

The Power of Product Inserts

Once you have a good product, the next part to focus on are product inserts. An insert is one of the best ways to get more reviews on Amazon and it cost almost nothing to implement.

Here are the top 3 benefits of putting a product insert in your packaging:

1 – More (likely) positive reviews

2 – Build your own email list. This is 100% crucial in launching a 7-figure brand, especially if you want to have full control of your income once you expand outside FBA and into your own website.

3 – Collected emails can be used as "lookalike audience" for FB Pixel and Google Tag Data. This makes running ads so much more profitable for your business.

How to Create a Customer Review Generating Insert

A – Always start with a "thank you" message. A simple thank you is often enough but you can also put 1-2 sentences in there and tell them how grateful you are for their patronage.

B – Give them discount codes or anything of value. You have two choices here, you can either give them a coupon code or you can ask them to go to your website and download some kind of report/eBook/template or anything that can be of value to them.

C – Ask for a review and give them a short and clear instruction on how to put theirs on Amazon. Never ever blatantly ask for a "positive review" as this is against Amazon's terms of service.

D – If your product is a bit on the technical side, give them some additional instructions on how to use the product so they can maximize its use.

E – Put your website URL on your inserts.

F – Put your social media @s on your inserts as well.

Here are some good examples to learn from:

Bonus Info: How to Use Amazon Coupons for More Sales and Higher Search Rankings

One of the easiest way to get more sales is by utilizing Amazon Coupons. Yes, it does cost money to run coupons but it's definitely worth the investment since you'll get a boost in both best-seller rankings and also in your organic search terms.

How It Works

For every coupon redeemed, you are required to pay at least $0.60 (cents) to Amazon.

In addition, you can offer 2 types of coupons. The first one is a discount percentage and the second one is a dollar discount. If the product is under $50, then use $ off coupon. If the product is more than $50, then use percentage off coupon.

Your total coupon budget will depend on how much you can afford and how many coupons you want to offer.

Here's an example breakdown:

Coupon Budget = ($ or % Discount x Number of Coupons) + ($0.60 x Number of Coupons)

i.e. ($5 x 100 coupons = $500) + (0.60 x 100 = $60)
= $560 Total Coupon Budget (amount you have to prepare)

You don't really need to worry about promoting your coupon as well because Amazon will automatically apply this coupon to your listing.

Price: $129.99 & FREE Returns
Coupon ✓ $30.00 extra savings coupon applied at checkout. Details

Get $10 off instantly: Pay $119.99 upon approval for the Amazon Store Card.

In addition, Amazon has a coupon page where thousands of people visit everyday looking for deals to snatch.

https://www.amazon.com/Coupons/

Your product wil be included in that list thus giving you a boost in sales and in search rankings.

Visit this page for more info bout this:

https://sellercentral.amazon.com/gp/help/external/20218 9350?ref_=sdus_soa_pday_xscus_202189350&ld=SDUSF BADirect

P.S. If you're looking for more ways to boost your FBA Sales, kindly checkout my book AMAZON FBA SALES BOOST.

Chapter 6 - Amazon PPC for Beginners

Many people freak out about Pay Per Click. I did too when I was just getting started. But here's the good news, it's actually pretty simple, and anyone can run & set up their own ppc ads in less than 30 minutes.

Now, this a beginner's guide to Amazon PPC so I probably won't be able to give you everything you need to scale to a million dollars per year just from ads alone. However, what I'm going to give you is a framework that can help you understand how to run ads on Amazon. We'll discuss stuff like the basics of PPC, ACOS (what it is/how to compute it), and keyword targeting campaigns. I'll also show you what to do with the actual data you're going to receive after your initial test. In the last part, I'll show you how to set up your campaign and make the right bids for your keywords.

What is Amazon PPC?

Amazon Pay Per Click Advertising allows us to target any keywords that Amazon visitors are typing in the search bar. By targeting the right keywords, we will be able to get more sales, increase our organic rankings for the same keywords, achieve higher best-seller rankings, and also launch our product even without much media attention on our side.

ACoS – Advertising Cost of Sale

ACoS has got to be the most important metric when it comes to running Amazon PPC because it determines whether we are profitable or not.

The simplest way to explain this is this:

OUR ACoS SHOULD ALWAYS BE LOWER THAN OUR GROSS PROFIT MARGIN FOR US TO MAKE A POSITIVE ROI.

Highlight that or write that down.

OUR ACoS SHOULD ALWAYS BE LOWER THAN OUR GROSS PROFIT MARGIN FOR US TO MAKE A POSITIVE ROI.

If you achieved that, then you are profitable.

For example, if our projected profit margin is 40%, then our ACoS to breakeven should be 40% as well. You getting to 41% ACoS means you're already losing money. Having an ACoS of 25% means you are making 15% in NET PROFIT (40% Profit Margin – 25% ACoS). We'll discuss more on this later.

Two Types of Ad Targeting

1 - Automatic Targeting

For AT, you allow Amazon to choose the best keywords for you. This means all you really have to do is choose a bid price and wait for the results. I recommend this type of ad targeting only if you're willing to wait for the results and run the ad for at least 14-21 days without touching anything. For AT, Amazon has to adapt and find the best keywords for your ad and it does take time for the machine to learn what the good keywords are to target. Remember that Amazon will get the keywords mostly from your listing so you better have a highly optimized product listing before you run an automatic targeting ad campaign.

2 – Manual Targeting

For MT, we will be choosing the keywords that we want to target. If you already have a MASTER KEYWORD LIST that you already used in your listing and back-end keywords, then you won't have any issue with this anymore. If you need more help in building your keyword list, I recommend that you checkout my book Amazon Keyword Research.

3 Types of Manual Targeting

A – Exact Match

Using exact match shows your ad to the people who searched for the exact keyword you put on your campaign. For example, if you add keywords like "bamboo" "toothbrush" and "bamboo toothbrush" – then Amazon will show your ad to people who searched for "bamboo" or "toothbrush" or "bamboo toothbrush." This makes the amount of people you are targeting incredibly small, but highly qualified as potential customers for your product assuming that you are using the right keywords. Simply put: exact match keywords have the highest likelihood of product purchase but it also has the lowest amount of volume you can expect.

B – Broad Match

Using broad match allows you to get more volume because Amazon will usually add keywords that are related to your main keywords. For example, if you use "toothbrush" as part of your keyword, then Amazon will also automatically add other keywords like "tooth paste", "tooth whitening" or anything related to the keyword you input. This gets you more volume but it also lessens the probability of purchase because you are targeting slightly less relevant items to what you are selling.

C – Phrase Match

Using phrase match allows you to target search terms in different phrases.
This means you also get to target phrases with added keywords before and after your main keyword. It also targets variations like misspellings, singulars, plurals, and abbreviations.

For example, if you target keywords like "toothbrush" and "bamboo toothbrush" – then Amazon may also include other keywords like:

"organic bamboo toothbrush"
"bamboo toothbrush holder"
"premium bamboo toothbrush"

Using phrase match allows you to target related keywords which balances both volume and audience targeting.

Sooooo... What type ad should you run?

I recommend that you skip broad match for now and run 2 different ads for exact match and phrase match, and then run 1 automatic ad as well for testing purposes.

Calculating Your Gross Profit Margin

This is the formula for calculating your Gross Profit Margin.

Product Price – (Cost of Goods Sold + FBA Fees) = Profit Margin Unit/Product Price

Product Price – The price of the product on Amazon

Cost of Goods Sold – This includes manufacturing, shipping, freight forwarder, VAT, coupons, etc.

FBA Fees – This includes referral fees, FBA fees, and storage fees

For example:

$45 (Product Price) – ($20 COGS + $10 FBA FEES) = $15 (Profit Unit)/45 (Product Price)

= 33.33% Gross Profit Margin

Remember: **YOUR ACoS SHOULD BE LOWER THAN YOUR GROSS PROFIT MARGIN FOR YOU TO MAKE POSITIVE ROI.**

If your Amazon PPC data shows that you have an ACoS of 20%, then in this case, you are making a 13.33% Net Profit Margin (33.33% - 20%).

If you are selling a $45 product, then calculate the 13.33% margin and that will be your NET PROFIT. ($45 x 0.1333) = $5.85 NET PROFIT.

In my opinion, a good NET PROFIT MARGIN is at the 10%-30% range. But this all still depends on how much money you want to make and how many units you are selling. If I'm selling 1 million pieces of my products every month, then I wouldn't mind having a net profit of $1 per product. *That's $1,000,000 per month NET for you math geniuses out there.* In that case, the percentage wouldn't really matter as much as the actual profit.

Note: Check this out if you need an FBA Profit Calculator.

https://junglescout.grsm.io/fbacalculator

Amazon PPC as Long-Term Strategy

Obviously, you want to make as much profit as possible so you can make PPC worth the time and effort. But you also have to look at it long-term and see its potential effect on your brand as a whole. If you're running PPC and you're only breaking even, you may second guess your decisions and you might stop running all your campaigns. But if you look at it long-term, you'll quickly realize that even at breakeven, the ads still have positive effects on your best-seller and search engine rankings thus increasing your organic/free sales. PPC is an essential aspect of your Amazon business and it's something that you should do long-term.

What to do with the results?

So, you've been running your ads for 2 weeks and you haven't touched a single thing about it – that's good because you're just letting the machines do the work.

At the end of week 2, only these 3 things may happen:

1 – BREAKEVEN

This is making your organic sales grow so just keep running the ads!

2 - ACOS IS HIGHER THAN PROFIT MARGIN (LOSS)

If you are at -20% ROI, then cut the ads and move on to creating a different one. If 1-2 sales could make you breakeven or positive ROI, then just keep running the ads for 2 more weeks and re-evaluate again after.

3 - ACOS IS LOWER THAN PROFIT MARGIN (PROFIT)

Increase your budget by 10% every week but watch your ACoS like a hawk. Expect the ACoS to rise up and make sure that you're still in the comfortable range when it comes to your NET PROFIT MARGIN.

NOTE:

Net Profit Margin* is the percentage derived from subtracting your "Gross Profit Margin" over your ACoS%. *Net Profit Margin and Gross Profit Margin is different**

Ways to Increase Your Net Profit Margin

1 – Lower Your Bid by 30%

You cannot always scale by sheer force so one of the best ways to increase your net profit margin is to actually spend less money on ads. The first thing that you can do to increase your profit margin is to lessen your expenses by lowering your bids. Don't do it aggressively though. If you are already making positive ROI, then start lowering your bids by at least 5% in the first week. Then if you're still making the same percentage of positive ROI, then lower it again by another 5% and so on until you hit 30% lower bid. At that point, you probably won't be able to get as much traffic if you continue lowering your bid unless you started with an incredibly high bid.

2 – Create the Same Ad With 30% Lower Bid

If you don't want to mess up an ad that's already making positive ROI, then you can just create another ad with the *same everything*. Same ad copy, same product, same keywords, same type of campaign, etc. The only difference this time is the amount of your bid. This time, bid 30% lower than your original bid and then run the ads for 2 weeks to see if you'll have the same positive results.

3 – Negotiate with Your Suppliers

From this point forward, every single cent you save on your sourcing directly goes to your net profit. For example, if you were able to re-negotiate your per unit price from $5 to $4.50 and you usually order 1,000 units per month, then you're basically putting an additional $500 on your pocket just for the product sourcing savings alone. I don't know about you but I'd love to have an extra $500 without any additional work every month. The more you grow, the more you'll be able to negotiate with your supplier and get as much savings as possible.

4 – Change Your Shipping Method

Another way to save money is by changing your shipping method. If shipping by AIR cost too much, then ship the other half by SEA. This will save you hundreds if not thousands of dollars that you could then add to your bottom line.

5 – Increase Your Price

Always test your price in a month to month basis. A small $1 increase in price probably won't hurt your sales figures that much and you'll also be able to make more money (again, without much additional work on your part. This is quite honestly the easiest way to make more profit from your current inventory. Always test the price and make sure that you do it in a semi long-term basis. Thirty (30) days is a good starting point for you to get a more accurate data.

Technical Set Up

I'm putting this in the last part because quite honestly, it's the easiest part. Everyone can set up a campaign in literally 20 minutes or less. The more important part is what to actually do with your campaigns and how to analyze the results which you already learned in this chapter.

How to Set Up a Campaign

Step 1 – Log in to your Amazon Seller Central, go to Advertising and hover to Campaign Manager.

Step 2 – Click the Create Campaign button and choose Sponsored Product Ads.

Sponsored Products

Promote products to shoppers actively
searching with related keywords or
viewing similar products on Amazon.

Continue

Step 3 – Name your campaign as "Product Name + MT1 or AT1" depending on what type of campaign you are doing.

Choose between Automatic Targeting and Manual Targeting.

Step 4 – Select the start date and end date of your campaign. You can always change this if you want to. For now, choose a start and end date of between 2-3 weeks.

Step 5 – Choose your daily budget. I recommend that you start with at least $20 per day so you can get data faster.

Step 6 – For the bidding strategy, I only use "Dynamic Bids – Down Only" where Amazon will bid a lower bid if it makes more sense to do so. This helps you get more traffic for your money without overspending on bids.

Step 6 – Select 1 product that you want to advertise by copying and pasting the ASIN of the product.

Products ⓘ

Search   Enter list   Upload

🔍 Search by product name, ASIN, or SKU	Q

Step 7 – Set your default bid. Most gurus would say that you should bid at a higher price first so you can get traffic faster and they wouldn't be wrong in giving you that advice. But personally, I like to play it safe and bid for at least 30% lower than what Amazon recommends.

Automatic Targeting

● Set default bid
    $ 0.75

○ Set bids by targeting group   New

Set your bids by targeting group and bid 20%-30% lower than what Amazon recommends.

Match type ⑦	Suggested bid ⑦	Keyword bid ⑦
Exact	$0.45 Apply ⑦ $0.42 - $0.65	$0.40
Phrase	$2.20 Apply ⑦ $2.00 - $2.20	$1.80
Exact	$0.50 Apply ⑦ $0.40 - $0.93	$0.35

Step 7.1 – If you're doing Manual Targeting, all you have to do is upload your keyword list file to Amazon and those

will be included in the targeting. You can also copy and paste those keywords in the **Enter List** part if you choose to do so.

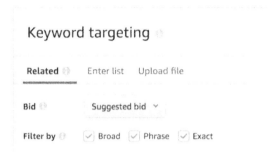

I recommend that you skip **broad match** if you already have hundreds or thousands of keywords on your list.

Step 8 – Click Launch Campaign and wait for approval.

Run the ads for two weeks without touching anything and then evaluate the results using the strategies I laid out in this chapter.

Conclusion

There you have it. A step by step guide on starting and launching your own Amazon FBA business.

Let me give you some action steps that you need to take:

Step 1 – Set up your Amazon account and do all the foundational stuff that we talk about in chapter 1.

Step 2 – Start looking for potential problems to solve and potential products to source. Make sure that you follow the criteria I laid out perfect for those who are just starting out in this business.

Step 3 – Look for suppliers that you can work with on a long-term basis.

Step 4 – Set up your Amazon listing so you can start getting orders for your product/s.

Step 5 – Do a minimal product launch by gathering real reviews and using Amazon PPC to get the initial traction needed to succeed.

Step 6 – Run PPC ads, evaluate the right action steps after the initial test, and then scale your net profit by either lowering your expenses and/or increasing your gross profit.

....

One Last Word

It's a proven fact that only a few people who buy any type of information products use what they learned from what they read or study.

I don't know the exact figure but I would assume that the action takers would only be at around 5% based on the buy to review ratio I get on my books. Heck, it's probably even lower than that.

My question to you is this.

Do you want to be part of the top 5% who will take action or will you be one of those who just gathered information and never did anything about it? I hope you choose to be part of the top 5%. That would be better for you, for your family, and for the world.

I wish you all the best in this amazing Amazon journey,

- Red

P.S. There's a favor on the next page ☺

Review Request

If you like this book and it helped you in some way or another, kindly post a review on Amazon.com. Reviews are the lifeblood of every author out there and it helps in sharing the message. I appreciate you and I look forward to hearing from you soon. Good luck with your business and I wish you all the success in the world.

OTHER FBA BOOKS

AMAZON FBA Step by Step – to help you get started with Amazon FBA and arbitrage (the basics)

FBA Product Research 101 – an in-depth guide to product research

Amazon Keyword Research 101 – an in-depth guide to Amazon keyword research

FBA Product Sourcing Blueprint – a step by step blueprint on sourcing products and shipping it to Amazon/your preferred destination

Amazon FBA Sales Boost – 33 little tricks to triple your Amazon sales

Million Dollar Ecommerce – how to build an ecommerce brand outside Amazon.

These are also available as audiobooks.

You can find the whole series here:

https://www.amazon.com/gp/product/B086QZCJQQ

Printed in Great Britain
by Amazon